First World War
and Army of Occupation
War Diary
France, Belgium and Germany

9 DIVISION
3 Lowland Brigades
Queen's Own Cameron Highlanders
9th Battalion.
1 April 1919 - 30 September 1919

WO95/1776/13

The Naval & Military Press Ltd
www.nmarchive.com
Published in association with The National Archives

Published by

The Naval & Military Press Ltd

Unit 10 Ridgewood Industrial Park,

Uckfield, East Sussex,

TN22 5QE England

Tel: +44 (0) 1825 749494

www.naval-military-press.com

www.nmarchive.com

This diary has been reprinted in facsimile from the original. Any imperfections are inevitably reproduced and the quality may fall short of modern type and cartographic standards.

© **Crown Copyright**
Images reproduced by permission of The National Archives, London, England, 2015.

Contents

Document type	Place/Title	Date From	Date To
Heading	Lowland (Late 9th) Division 3rd Lowland Bde 9 Scottish Rifles 1919 Apr-1919 Sep From 27 Bde 9 Div		
War Diary	Benrath Germany	01/04/1919	30/04/1919
War Diary	Benrath	01/05/1919	30/06/1919
War Diary	Neurath	01/07/1919	31/08/1919
War Diary	Neurath Germany	01/09/1919	30/09/1919

LOWLAND (LATE 9th) DIVISION

3rd LOWLAND BDE

9 SCOTTISH RIFLES

1919 APR – 1919 SEP

from 27 BDE 9 DIV

9 Scottish Rifles

Army Form C.2118.

W.46

WAR DIARY

(Erase heading not required.)

Instructions regarding War Diaries and Intelligence Summaries are contained in F.S. Regs. Part II. and the Staff Manual respectively. Title pages will be prepared in manuscript.

Place	Date	Hour	Summary of Events and Information	Remarks and references to Appendices
Benrath, GERMANY.	1919. Apr. 1st.		"A" & "C" Coys. struck off all duties for one month for training. "B" and "D" Coys., take over duties.	
	2nd.		"A" & "C" Coy., on training. 6 Officers reported for duty.	
	3rd.		"A" & "C" Coy., on training. Lieut. Gilchrist and Lieut. Borland to dispersal camp. 2/Lt. Bolt from leave.	
	4th.		"A" & "C" Coy., on Route March.	
	5th.		Kit inspection, lecture etc., in Coy. Billets. 2/. R.J.Ross reported for duty.	
	6th.		Church Parades - compulsory.	
	7th.		Training of "A" & "C" Coy. - day and night outposts.	
	8th.		Training of "A" & "C" Coy., as usual. Lecture by Lt. HALLAM on "Advantages and liabilities of re-engagement in the Post Bellum Army." Result of "Best Coy." Competition:- "B" Coy. S.R.2; 90th Fd. Coy. R.E.- Nil.	
	9th.		Training of "A" & "C" Coys., as usual. 2/Lt. Harley to Dispersal Camp.	
	10th.		Training of "A" & "C" Coy., as usual. Capt. J. Mathieson to Dispersal Camp.	
	11th.		Training "A" & "C" Coy., as usual, on Benrath Football Ground. Capt. Renshaw and Lieut. Crawford reported for duty.	
	12th.		Kit inspections, cleaning up billets etc. 2/Lt. Burrows to Disp. Camp.	
	13th.		Usual Church Parades. Lieut. Gardiner from here.	
	14th.		Training - all available Subalterns and O.Rs.	

Army Form C. 2118.

WAR DIARY
or
~~INTELLIGENCE SUMMARY~~

(Erase heading not required.)

Instructions regarding War Diaries and Intelligence Summaries are contained in F.S. Regs., Part II. and the Staff Manual respectively. Title pages will be prepared in manuscript.

Place	Date	Hour	Summary of Events and Information	Remarks and references to Appendices
	15th.		Training as yesterday. Lt. Col., Jack from leave.	
	16th.		Training as usual. Lt. Col., Jack assumed command of Bde. 2/Lt. Stevenson on Course. Lieut. Houston and 2/Lt. Calder to Disp. Camp.	
	17th.		Usual training.	
	18th.		Good Friday. Holiday except for C. of E. Parade.	
	19th.		Usual training. Capt. G.W.Kindersley to Disp. Camp. Change of Command:- Capt. Bacon M.C. to "B" Coy. - Capt. Dewar to "C" Coy. - Major Mackinlay M.C. to "D" Coy.	
	20th.		Usual Church Parades.	
	21st.		Easter Monday. Holiday. 2/Lt. Hamilton on Course.	
	22nd.		Usual Training.	
	23rd.		Usual Training.	
	24th.		Usual Training. Lt. Moon to T.M.B.	
	25th.		Training as usual. Capt. Dewar on leave. Capt. Renshaw to L.T.M.B.	
	26th.		Kit inspections, cleaning up billets, etc.	
	27th.		Church Parades. Capt. Bacon on leave. Capt. Gilmour from leave. 2/Lt. Buchanan to Disp. Camp.	
	28th.		Usual Training.	
	29th.		Training. 2/Lt. Wotherspoon assumed command of "A" Coy.	
	30th.		Training. Lt. Col. Lumsden assumed command of Brigade vice Lt. Col. Jack, evacuated Sick.	

Innes Hurndar
Major,
Commanding 9th Bn. Cameronians (Scottish Rifles.)

Army Form C. 2118.

WAR DIARY or INTELLIGENCE SUMMARY.
(Erase heading not required.)

GSR

Instructions regarding War Diaries and Intelligence Summaries are contained in F. S. Regs., Part II. and the Staff Manual respectively. Title pages will be prepared in manuscript.

Place	Date	Hour	Summary of Events and Information	Remarks and references to Appendices
Benrath	1/5/19		Major Macaulay assumed command of the Battalion and Lieut G. Hearn assumed command of "D" Coy.	
	2/5/19		Training as usual. Blowing up drills. 2nd Lt Johnson took over company as Adjutant, Major Dempsey went on leave	
	3/5/19		Rate of Exchange for month of May 10 marks = 3/3	
	4/5/19		L.G.L.M. for Cpl Donyard. W.O work. Lt Pte Merchant	
	5/5/19		Officers Riding Class. Training as usual	
	6/5/19		Training as usual	
	7/5/19		New express train for other ranks from Cologne to Calais in 16 hrs	
	8/5/19		Court of Inquiry held at Hoffhausen Post to inquire into the shooting of Albert Muntz	
	9/5/19		Training as usual 2dLt Hamilton went on leave to UK	
	10/5/19		Church parade as usual	
	11/5/19		Capt Dewar returns from leave	
	12/5/19		Training as usual	
	13/5/19		" " "	
	14/5/19		" " "	

Army Form C. 2118.

WAR DIARY
or
INTELLIGENCE SUMMARY.
(Erase heading not required.)

Instructions regarding War Diaries and Intelligence Summaries are contained in F. S. Regs., Part II. and the Staff Manual respectively. Title pages will be prepared in manuscript.

Place	Date	Hour	Summary of Events and Information	Remarks and references to Appendices
Benrath	15/5/19		Capt. Bacon returns from Leave. 2/Lieut. Penny goes on leave	
	16/5/19		Training fit. Inspection of Billets. 2/Lt. Coulson relinquishes command as a/Adj. Capt. Bacon assumes command.	
	17/5/19		Major Dumper returns from leave	
	18/5/19		Training as usual. Officers Riding Class	
	19/5/19		Mess Meeting held at 14.00 hrs.	
	20/5/19		Leave stops temporarily owing to the question of Peace Terms	
	21/5/19		Capt. J. Coulson took over command of B & Coy. 2/Lt Balk relinquishes command of B Coy from that date	
	22/5/19		Training as usual. 2/Lt Balk takes over duties of M. Evening Officer	
	23/5/19		Officers early morning parade for Running Sports, remaining all men employed on Battalion Duties	
	24/5/19		Church Parade as usual	
	25/5/19		2/Lt. Wortheryton assumes temporary command as temporary transport officer	
	26/5/19		The Captain of the day again resumed duties from this date	
	27/5/19		Officers early morning parade, Riding class, men employed on Battalion duties	
	28/5/19		Strike of all works in Benrath, agitators deported to Köln. Twenty of the workmen deported over the frontier to Dusseldorf, pass labels from Heart given, given one day's rations.	

Army Form C. 2118.

WAR DIARY
or
INTELLIGENCE SUMMARY.
(Erase heading not required.)

Instructions regarding War Diaries and Intelligence Summaries are contained in F. S. Regs., Part II. and the Staff Manual respectively. Title pages will be prepared in manuscript.

Place	Date	Hour	Summary of Events and Information	Remarks and references to Appendices
Benrath	29/5/19		General Holiday — Strike still in progress but everything quiet.	
	30/5/19		Strike still in progress. Leaders still being arrested.	
	31/5/19		Strikers still refuse to return to work. Some men returned to duty in Electrical works, situation quiet	

Dewwey Hoos Lt. Col.
for
Comdg. 9th Bn. Camerons (Scottish Rifles)

A.291
Army Form C. 2118.

2nd Bde.
Low row
9th Scot. R.

WAR DIARY
or
INTELLIGENCE SUMMARY.
(Erase heading not required.)

Instructions regarding War Diaries and Intelligence Summaries are contained in F. S. Regs., Part II. and the Staff Manual respectively. Title pages will be prepared in manuscript.

Place	Date	Hour	Summary of Events and Information	Remarks and references to Appendices
BENRATH.	1/6/19.		Strike settled men back to work, usual church parades & men allowed anywhere within the Battalion Area.	
	2/6/19.		Orderly Room moved to Schloss School. Training as usual.	
	3/6/19.		Kings Birthday. Parade & March Past Brigadier. Sports in the Schloss Grounds in afternoon.	
	4/6/19.		Parades as usual.	
	5/6/19.		Subalterns early morning parade, & usual training.	
	6/6/19.		Usual early morning parade & inspection of billets by C.O. A/Capt. D.N.Maclachlan joined 5/6/19. From 5/6th.Bn,2nd Lt is appointed A/Adjt.	
	7/6/19.		Usual Church Services. Capt.Bacon takes over command of Lt."A".Coy. Capt.Johnston takes over temporary command of Lt."B".Coy.	
	8/6/19.		Whit Monday observed as a holiday.	
	9/6/19.		Early morning parades, Squad Drill,Musketry,Recreational Training. Lecture to Subalterns by Major J.J.Dempsey.M.C. Lecture 14-15.(Change of pay system).	
	10/6/19.		Capt.Johnston relinquishes command of Lt."B".Coy. & takes over command of "A". Lieut.S.Leckie takes over command of Lt."B".Coy.	
	11/6/19.		Lt.Patience is transferred from "D".Coy. to "B".Coy.	

Army Form C. 2118.

WAR DIARY
or
INTELLIGENCE SUMMARY.
(Erase heading not required.)

Instructions regarding War Diaries and Intelligence Summaries are contained in F. S. Regs., Part II. and the Staff Manual respectively. Title pages will be prepared in manuscript.

Place	Date	Hour	Summary of Events and Information	Remarks and references to Appendices
Benrath.	11/6/19.		Lts. Rowland & Ross. are struck off all Battalion Duties whilst employed on Summary Court.	
	12/6/19.		Increase of Baggage for Officers of Armies of Occupation. Training as usual.	
	13/6/19.		C. Ds. inspection parade & inspection of billets.	
	14/6/19.		Church Parade as usual.	
	15/6/19.		Usual Training. Early morning parade & Musketry, Drill, Recreational Training etc.	
	16/6/19.		Lecture at Hilden. Divisional Commander calls to see Battalion Area.	
	17/6/19.		No Training. B. & C. Coys. move billets over beside "A". & "D". Coy.	
	18/6/19.		Standing By in the event of Peace not being signed.	
	19/6/19		"Corpus Christi". Early morning parade. Extention given for signing Peace.	
	20/6/19.		Lecture at Hilden by Rev. J. R. P. Slater, D. D. of EDINBURGH.	
	21/6/19.		Inspection of Billets by C.O. & also Inspection of Battalion in Battle Order.	
	22/6/19.		Usual Church Parades.	
	23/6/19.		Training same as usual.	
	24/6/19.		Standing by to advance if necessary.	
	25/6/19.		Range Practices at URDEMBACH. Rate of exchange 10. Marks = 2/9.	
	26/6/19.		Carrying of Revolvers by Officers ceases to-day. Training as usual.	

Army Form C. 2118.

WAR DIARY
or
INTELLIGENCE SUMMARY.
(Erase heading not required)

Instructions regarding War Diaries and Intelligence Summaries are contained in F.S. Regs. Part II. and the Staff Manual respectively. Title pages will be prepared in manuscript.

Place	Date	Hour	Summary of Events and Information	Remarks and references to Appendices
Berrath.	27/6/19.		Training as usual.	
	28/6/19.		Inspection of Billets by C.O. Peace signed, 101 Guns fired at COLOGNE.	
	29/6/19.		Church Parades as usual.	
	30/6/19.		Commencement of Education Classes.	

INCREASE.		DECREASE.		TOTAL STRENGTH.	
Off.	O.R.	Off.	O.R.	Off.	O.R.
1.	2.	4.	17.	29.	264.

M Decuney Major.
Cmdg. 9th. Bn. The Cameronians.(Scottish Rifles).

Army Form C. 2118.

WAR DIARY
or
INTELLIGENCE SUMMARY.
(Erase heading not required.)

9 S.R.

Place	Date	Hour	Summary of Events and Information	Remarks and references to Appendices
NEURATH.	1/7/19.		Range Practise.	
	2/7/19.		"B" & "C" Coys. move from Arbisterheim to Schloss, Benrath.	
	3/7/19.		Holiday for all ranks and arrival of Draft from England. 150 O.R.	
	4/7/19.		Inspection of draft by C.O. Usual training for all ranks.	
	5/7/19.		Church Parade.	
	6/7/19.		Battalion preparing for move to BEDBURG. No training.	
	7/7/19.		53rd Rifle Brigade Batt. relieved this Battn. at BENRATH.	
	8/7/19.		Battalion moved to BEDBURG.	
	9/7/19.		Training under Company arrangements.	
	10/7/19.		Traning. Rifle exercises, Musketry, &c.	
	11/7/19.		Cleaning up Camp.	
	12/7/19.		Training under Company arrangements.	
	13/7/19.		Battalion moved to NEURATH.	
	14/7/19.		Training and Baths.	
	15/7/19.		Route March.	
	16/7/19.		Usual training. Musketry, Rifle Drill, &c.	

WAR DIARY
or
INTELLIGENCE SUMMARY.
(Erase heading not required.)

Army Form C. 2118.

Place	Date	Hour	Summary of Events and Information	Remarks and references to Appendices
NEURATH.	17/7/19		Educational parade under Education Officer.	
	18/7/19		Training.	
	19/7/19		Cleaning of billets and inspection by C.O.	
	20/7/19		Church parades.	
	21/7/19		Education training.	
	22/7/19		Range Practice.	
	23/7/19		Education parades and inspection of Small Box Respirators.	
	24/7/19		Education and Inspection of Respirators of C & D Coys. by Batt. Gas N.C.O.	
	25/7/19		Range Practice.	
	26/7/19		Training. Lecture on War Saving Certificates, by Major Wade.	
	27/7/19		Church Parades.	
	28/7/19		Training.	
	29/7/19		Battalion and billets inspected by Sir Wm. Robertson, G.C.B.,G.C.M.G.,K.C.V.O.,D.S.O.,A.D.C..	
	30/7/19		Educational Training.	
	31/7/19		Range Practice.	

[signature] Lt.Col.
Commanding 9th Bn. The Cameronians (Scottish Rifles).

Army Form C. 2118.

WAR DIARY
or
INTELLIGENCE SUMMARY.
(Erase heading not required.)

Instructions regarding War Diaries and Intelligence Summaries are contained in F. S. Regs., Part II. and the Staff Manual respectively. Title pages will be prepared in manuscript.

Place	Date	Hour	Summary of Events and Information	Remarks and references to Appendices
NEURATH.	1-8-19.		P.&M.Book introduced. Educational Classes.	
	2-8-19.		Range Practice.	
	3-8-19.		Church Parades.	
	4-8-19.		Bank Holiday. (Military Training Suspended.)	
	5-8-19.		Musketry Practice for Rifle Meeting.	
	6-8-19.		Lecture on Venereal Disease by Revd.G.H.HEASLET. B.A. Cinema Show.	
	"		Football Match against 159th Regt.D'Infanterie d'Alpine.	
	7-8-19.		Educational Classes. Lecture on Glass Making by Revd.P.S. ELEY. B.A.	
	8-8-19.		Range Practice. Field Dressings withdrawn.	
	9-8-19.		Usual Parades.	
	10-8-19.		Church Parades.	
	11-8-19.		Range Practice.	
	12-8-19.		Usual Training.	
	13-8-19.		Usual Training.	
	14-8-19.		Educational Classes. Lecture by Lt.A.H.Groves, Lowland Div.M.T.Coy. to all Apprentices in this Battalion.	

A6945 Wt.W14142/M1160 350,000 12/16 D. D. & L. Forms/C./2118/14

Army Form C. 2118.

WAR DIARY
or
INTELLIGENCE SUMMARY.
(Erase heading not required.)

Instructions regarding War Diaries and Intelligence
Summaries are contained in F. S. Regs., Part II.
and the Staff Manual respectively. Title pages
will be prepared in manuscript.

Place	Date	Hour	Summary of Events and Information	Remarks and references to Appendices
NEURATH.	15-8-19.		Practices for Rifle Meeting.	
	16-8-19.		Usual Parades. Football Match against 159th.Regt.D'Infanterie D'Alpine at GUSTORF.	
	17-8-19.		Church Parades.	
	18-8-19.		Range Practice. Orders received that the Battalion will proceed about 25th. with Western Division to CURRAGH IRELAND.	
	19-8-19.		Educational Parade.	
	20-8-19.		Joint Sports with 63rd.Field Coy.R.E. Divisional Staff, Brigade Staff, French Generals & friends attended.	
	21-8-19.		Range Practice. 7 Horses proceeded to COLOGNE en route for U.K.	
	22-8-19.		Usual Training.	
	23-8-19.		Usual Training.	
	24-8-19.		Divine Services. Orders received that move to U.K. is postponed until 2nd.Septr.	
	25-8-19.		Training under Company Arrangements.	
	26-8-19.		Range Practice.	
	27-8-19.		March.- Route. FRIMMERSDORF NEUENHAUSEN - ALLRATH.	
	28-8-19.		Range Practice.	

A6945 Wt. W1422/M1160 350,000 12/16 D. D. & L. Forms/C/2118/14.

Army Form C. 2118.

WAR DIARY
or
INTELLIGENCE SUMMARY.
(Erase heading not required.)

Instructions regarding War Diaries and Intelligence Summaries are contained in F. S. Regs., Part II. and the Staff Manual respectively. Title pages will be prepared in manuscript.

Place	Date	Hour	Summary of Events and Information	Remarks and references to Appendices
NEURATH.	28-8-19.		Football Match against 1/8th.Scottish Rifles at KONIGSHOVEN. Score. 9th.S.R. 7 Goals. 1/8th.S.R. 1 Goal.	
	29-8-19.		Training under Company Arrangements. All horses handed over to 50th.Bde & mules to D.A.C.	
	30-8-19.		Cleaning and preparing to move.	
	31-8-19.		Divine Services. All vehicles & baggage entrained at HAREF en route for AINTREE via ANTWERP. Battalion Parade. Farewell to Brig.General.E.S.Girdwood, C.B. C.M.G.	

(signature)
Lt.Col.
Cmdg.9th.Bn.The Cameronians.(Scottish Rifles.)

WAR DIARY
or
INTELLIGENCE SUMMARY.
(Erase heading not required.)

Army Form C. 2118.

9 Sco. Rif[e]

Place	Date	Hour	Summary of Events and Information	Remarks and references to Appendices
NEURACH GERMANY.	1/9/19.		Battn. prepares to move to U.K. with Western Divn. on the 2nd. Sept.	
	2/9/19		Battn leaves "NEURATH" GERMANY for U.K. at 10:00 hours & marched to HARFF. Gen. Tudor C.B. C.M.G. & Staff , Brig. Gen. Girdwood C.B. C.M.G. & Staff awaited the arrival of the Battn at HARFF Station. The Battn was formed up in the square and Gen. Tudor delivered his farewell speech and expressed his regret at the Battn leaving the Divn. The band of the 1/4th R.S.F. played stirring music & amidst cheers from all those who gathered at the stations the train moved off at 11"00 hours. ROUTE:- DUREN, HUY, CHAMEROI, CHISLINGHEM, MERRIS, CALAIS, DOVER, NORTHHAMPTON, HOLYHEAD & DUBLIN.	
			At Duren the Cavalry Regt. 12th Lancers, 9th Dragoon Gds. & 11th Hussars joined the train. Halt Repas HUY about 21:00 hours, men had a hot meal.	
	3/9/19		Halt Repas CHISLINGHEM men had a warm meal. Last halt MERRIS. The Battn. arrived at CALAIS at 22"00 hours & marched to No.8 Rest Camp. Unloading party under Lts. Wood & Gardiner.	
	4/9/19		Battn leaves Rest Camp at 09"00 hours, embarks 12"00 hours. The Battn. Mascot "HANNIE" since October 1916 was not allowed on board and has been left in France. Disembark DOVER one hour later & marched to Rest Camp for the night.	
	5/9/19		Battn. entrains DOVER Station 10:30 hours. Train leaves & 11:45 hours. Halt Repas NORTHHAMPTON men have warm meal. On arriving at HOLYHEAD 10:30 hours the Battn. has warm meal & go straight on board boat.	
	6/9/19		The Battn. arrives DUBLIN 09:00 hours & entrains for "THE CURRAGH" 10:30 hours arriving 12:00 hours & marched to HARE PARK CAMP. Baggage etc. arrives in the evening.	
	7/9/19		Cleaning up of Billets. Divine Service in Y.M.C.A. HUT.	
	8/9/19		Early morning parade. Parades under Coy Commanders. Inlying Picquet consisting of 1 officer & 25 other ranks detailed daily in case of any riots etc.	
	9/9/19		Usual Parades. Football Match against 1/8th Sco. Rifs. SCORE 2-0 for this Battn.	
	10/9/19		do --do-- do do 1st do do	
	11-13/9/19			
	14/9/19		Divine Service in Y.M.C.A. HUT.	2 shets
	15/9/19 to 20/9/19		Usual Parades i.e. 10"00 to 10:30 hours Battn. under Adjt. for Drill & Handling of Arms. 10:30 to 11"00 hours Musketry, 11:00 to 12:30 hours under Coy Commanders.	

Army Form C. 2118.

WAR DIARY
or
INTELLIGENCE SUMMARY.
(Erase heading not required.)

Instructions regarding War Diaries and intelligence Summaries are contained in F. S. Regs., Part II. and the Staff Manual respectively. Title pages will be prepared in manuscript.

Place	Date	Hour	Summary of Events and Information	Remarks and references to Appendices
	21/9/19.		Divine Service in Y.M.C.A. Hut RATH CAMP.	
	22/9/19.		Usual Parades.	
	23/9/19.		Orders received that this Battalion is to be disbanded and all retainable men to be transferred to the 1st Battalion The Cameronians. All non-regular Officers except those who have volunteered for further service abroad have to be demobilized.	
	24/9/19.		Usual Parades.	
	25/9/19.		Usual Parades.	
	26/9/19.		172 Other Ranks transferred to the 1st Battalion. The undermentioned Officers proceeded for Dispersal. Capt. F. B. Munro. Lt. F. J. Deacon. Lt. D. Wood. Lt. G. Shearer. 2/Lt. J. W. Wotherspoon. 2/Lt. J. B. Clulow. 2/Lt. J. Gilchrist. 2/Lt. J. Stevenson.	
	27/9/19.		Lt. D. K. Hamilton proceeded for dispersal. Capt. J. B. W. Dewar, Lt. W. S. Crawford, & 2/Lt. G. A. Perrotti attached to 1st Battalion.	
	28/9/19.		Usual Church Parades.	
	29/9/19.		45 Other Ranks transferred to the 1st Battalion.	
	30/9/19.		17 " " " " " today thus leaving this Battalion with 35 Other Ranks who are detached i. c. Courses, Prison, Hospital etc. in GERMANY. These are being transferred to the 5/6th Battalion Scottish Rifles for record purposes. Here endeth the 9th Battalion The Cameronians (Scottish Rifles).	

STRENGTH. Officers.- 15. (2 in Hospital U. K. & 1 in hospital in Germany).

Lt. Col.,
Commanding 9th Battn. The Cameronians (Sco. Rif.)

www.ingramcontent.com/pod-product-compliance
Lightning Source LLC
Chambersburg PA
CBHW081511160426
43193CB00014B/2651